Susan Goodman • Sandy Hammer

ACTION BOOKS

PEOPLE AND PLACES

Published by
New Look Books
PO Box 864
Oxford
OX2 9YD

© New Look Books Ltd 1996, Reprinted 1997.

All rights reserved. No part of this publication may be reproduced, stored in a retrieval system, or transmitted, in any form or by any means, electronic, mechanical, photocopying, recording or otherwise, without the written permission of the publishers.

ISBN 1-901308-02-2

British Library Cataloguing in Publication Data.
A catalogue record for this book is available from the British Library.

Printed and bound in Great Britain.

People power

Here is a list of countries with their populations. Round each one to the nearest million.

Australia	17 100 000	17
Canada	26 600 000	
France	56 180 000	
Germany	79 070 000	
India	843 930 000	
Jamaica	2 400 000	
Japan	123 260 000	
Kenya	24 080 000	
Mexico	81 140 000	
China	1 114 000 000	
Pakistan	105 400 000	
Spain	39 540 000	
Sweden	8 500 000	
Taiwan	20 300 000	
USA	249 630 000	
UK	57 240 000	
South Africa	30 190 000	

DO YOU KNOW?
The world's population in 1996 was about 5,700,000,000. It is increasing by about 87 million a year, that's about 160 people a minute. There are about 150 million babies born a year, that's almost 300 a minute.

Alphabetics

Read these fascinating facts about alphabets and answer the questions below.

The alphabet for the English language has 26 letters. It is the most widely used alphabet in the world. It comes from the alphabet used by the ancient Romans when they wrote their language, Latin. Their alphabet had 23 letters. The letters J, U, and W were added much later.

There are over 60 other alphabets used around the world. Most of them have between 20 and 30 letters, but one used in Sri Lanka has over 50 letters.

Not all languages have alphabets. The Chinese do not write down the letter sounds of their words. Instead they draw a shape showing the idea of the whole word. They are called ideograms.

Cross out the incorrect words in the brackets.

(All, most, some) languages have alphabets.
(All, most, some) languages have more than 20 letters.
(All, most, some) alphabets come from the Latin alphabet.

See how many words you can find in the word

ALPHABET

10: good
20: very good
30: excellent

Lost languages

Rearrange the letters in each group to find the language.

- HUDCTUC → DUTCH
- CHERNRF → FRENCH
- NMEGRMAE → GERMAN
- WEHRBEB → HEBREW
- ENEHCSIEC → CHINESE
- SPINHASI → SPANISH
- KEEGR → GREEK
- PEEENAJSA → JAPANESE
- ILANTIA → ITALIAN
- ISSNRUA → RUSSIAN
- SGHIGELNH → ENGLISH
- EPROEUTPOSGTUU → PORTUGUESE
- AICARBA → ARABIC

DO YOU KNOW?
There are more than 4,000 languages spoken in the world. The most widely spoken is Mandarin Chinese with over 750 million speaking it. English is spoken by more than 350 million and Spanish by 250 million.

Holiday hotel

Look at the prices and read the hotel descriptions below. Decide which hotel is A, B, C.

Which week is most expensive at each hotel?

Which week is the cheapest at each hotel?

Find the difference in price between the most expensive and cheapest weeks for each hotel. Why do you think the prices change during the year?

	Name of hotel		
Date of departure	Paradise	Apollo	Stella
31 May — 6 Jun	469	402	334
7 Jun — 20 Jun	474	414	349
21 Jun — 4 Jul	489	425	359
5 Jul — 11 Jul	499	452	369
12 Jul — 18 Jul	509	479	379
19 Jul — 8 Aug	534	503	404
9 Aug — 15 Aug	529	498	399
16 Aug — 22 Aug	524	492	394
23 Aug — 5 Sep	519	485	379
6 Sep — 19 Sep	499	467	364
20 Sep — 3 Oct	464	442	324
4 Oct — 10 Oct	434	365	298

All prices are in £. Each price is per person for one week. It includes flight and hotel accommodation.

A. This family-run hotel has a swimming-pool and a pool-side snack bar.

B. Highly recommended hotel. The facilities include swimming-pool, gym, floodlit tennis courts and a beauty parlour.

C. The hotel has its own pool, bar and restaurant. Nearby there are tennis courts and a gym.

Travel time

Here is a train timetable for trains going from Smoke City to the seaside resort of Sun Beach. A few trains stop at the villages of Greenfields and Meadowlands.

Smoke City	Greenfields	Meadowlands	Sun Beach
0600	0645	----	0807
0732	0817	0847	0945
0850	----	----	1045
1000	----	----	1200
1145	1230	----	1353
1303	----	1418	1510
1436	1521	1551	1700
1642	----	----	1845
1845	----	----	2051
2036	----	2151	2249
2200	2245	2315	0027

John lives half an hour's drive from the station at Greenfields. If he leaves home at ten minutes to eight in the morning, which train will he miss? How long will he have to wait for the next train?

Wesley lives about the same distance from Greenfields and Meadowlands. It takes 30 minutes to drive to either village station. The time now is 8.10 a.m. Which station should he drive to so that he can get to Sun Beach as soon as possible?

Which Smoke City train has the shortest journey time to Sun Beach?

Desert test

WARNING: DO NOT READ THE NEXT PAGE UNTIL YOU HAVE ANSWERED THESE PROBLEMS.

Tick the correct box.

TRUE   FALSE

1. Deserts have no rain.
2. Deserts are always hot, except at night.
3. Camels are the only animals which can live in deserts.
4. Deserts are mainly sand.
5. There are no great rivers flowing in deserts.

The answer which at first looks the right one may not really be correct. The information on the next page will help you to decide which of the above statements are true.

NOW READ THE NEXT PAGE UPSIDE DOWN

DO YOU KNOW?
The driest desert in the world is the Atacama in Chile. It had no rain for 400 years until it rained in 1971.

Here are the desert answers.

1. Deserts have almost no rain but some deserts do have heavy storms one year and then no rain for many years. Geographers describe a desert as a place where there is less than 250mm of rain in an average year.

2. Most deserts are near the tropics and are very hot. Deserts further north, such as the Gobi on the borders with China, are hot in the summer but bitterly cold in the winter.

3. Deserts support all sorts of life other than camels. Some animals, such as the kangaroo rat and the gerbil, can survive with almost no water. Other animals sleep during the day and look for food in the cool of the night.

4. Most deserts have large stony areas. The Sahara, the largest desert in the world, is only one tenth sandy and most other deserts have less sand than that.

5. The Nile, the world's longest river, crosses the Sahara desert.

Sight-seeing

Look at the pictures showing famous sights in Western Europe. Read the information by each illustration of a famous building and draw a line to the capital city where it can be found.

Colosseum
An enormous open-air stadium used for chariot races and bloody fights between gladiators. Sometimes animals or people were hunted in the arena. At other times people were thrown to wild animals to be torn apart.

Big Ben
This is the bell on which hours are struck, inside the world's most famous clock, which stands beside the Houses of Parliament. The bell weighs almost 13½ tonnes, that's more than two large African elephants.

It was named after Sir Benjamin (Ben) Hall who was in charge of getting the bell up inside the tower.

Eiffel Tower
It was the tallest structure in the world until the New York skyscrapers were built. Now it and the skyscrapers are dwarfed by radio and television masts used for transmitting programmes.

It was built for the Paris Exhibition in 1889 by Alexandre-Gustave Eiffel. Originally it was 300.5 m high. Now with the addition of a TV antenna it is 320.75m.

Brandenburg Gate
It is in the capital city of a country which had been divided into two countries after the Second World War. The west and east of this country were united in 1990.

The Brandenburg Gate had stood on the boundary between the western and eastern sectors of this city.

Cool co-ordinates

Here is a map of Antarctica. Nearly all this area at the South Pole is covered with ice over three kilometres thick. The first explorer to reach the South Pole was Roald Amundsen, a Norwegian, who arrived there on 14 December 1911.

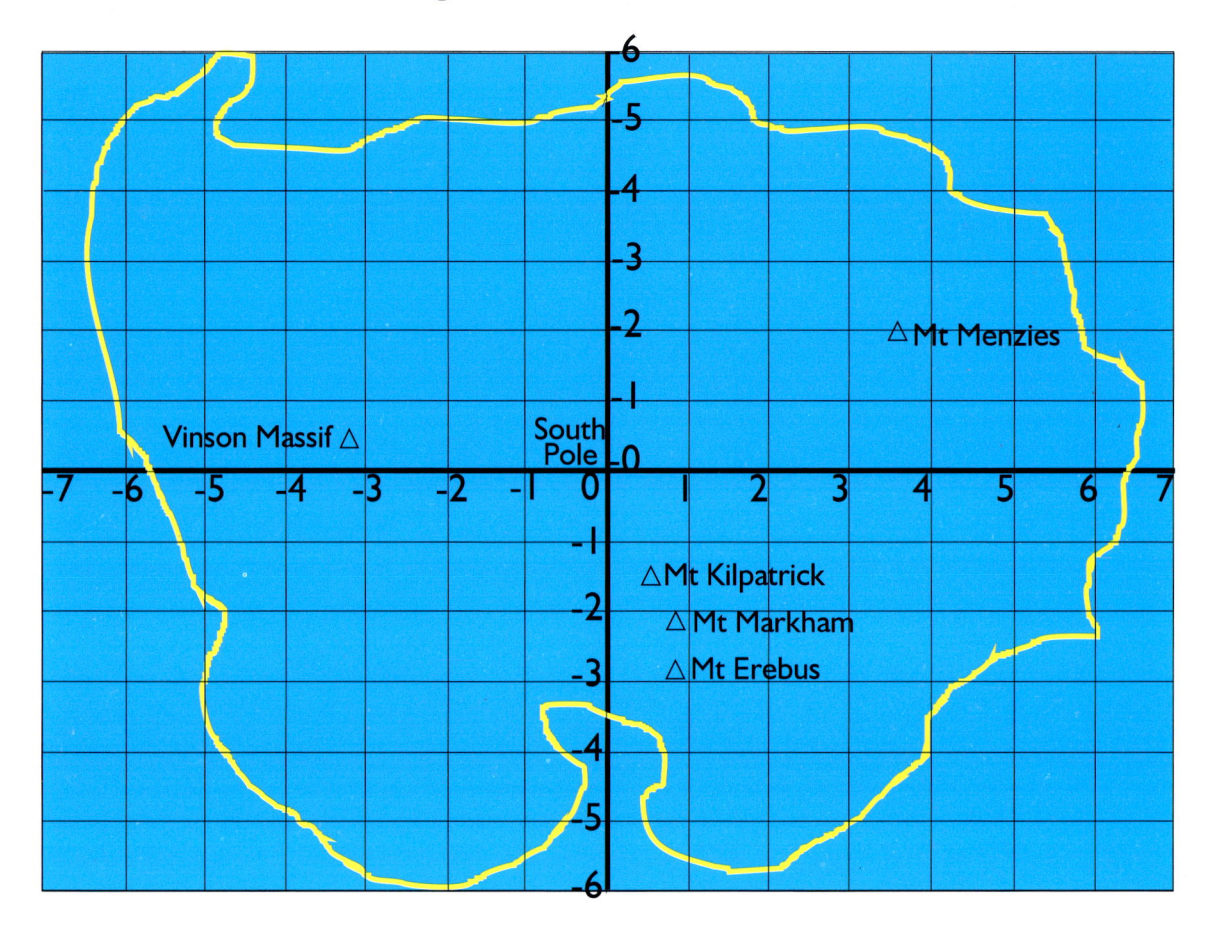

Pretend you are an explorer. Here is the route you take to the South Pole. List the mountains as you pass them.

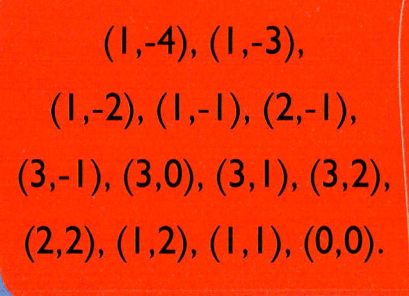

(1,-4), (1,-3), (1,-2), (1,-1), (2,-1), (3,-1), (3,0), (3,1), (3,2), (2,2), (1,2), (1,1), (0,0).

DO YOU KNOW?
The lowest recorded temperature in the world is -89.2°C at Vostok, Antarctica.

Freeze-up

Most of the Arctic is an enormous frozen ocean. The lands around it remain frozen and snow-covered much of the year. Polar bears, seals and walruses live here. In summer the top few centimetres of soil thaws, plants burst into growth and provide grazing for reindeer, caribou and musk ox.

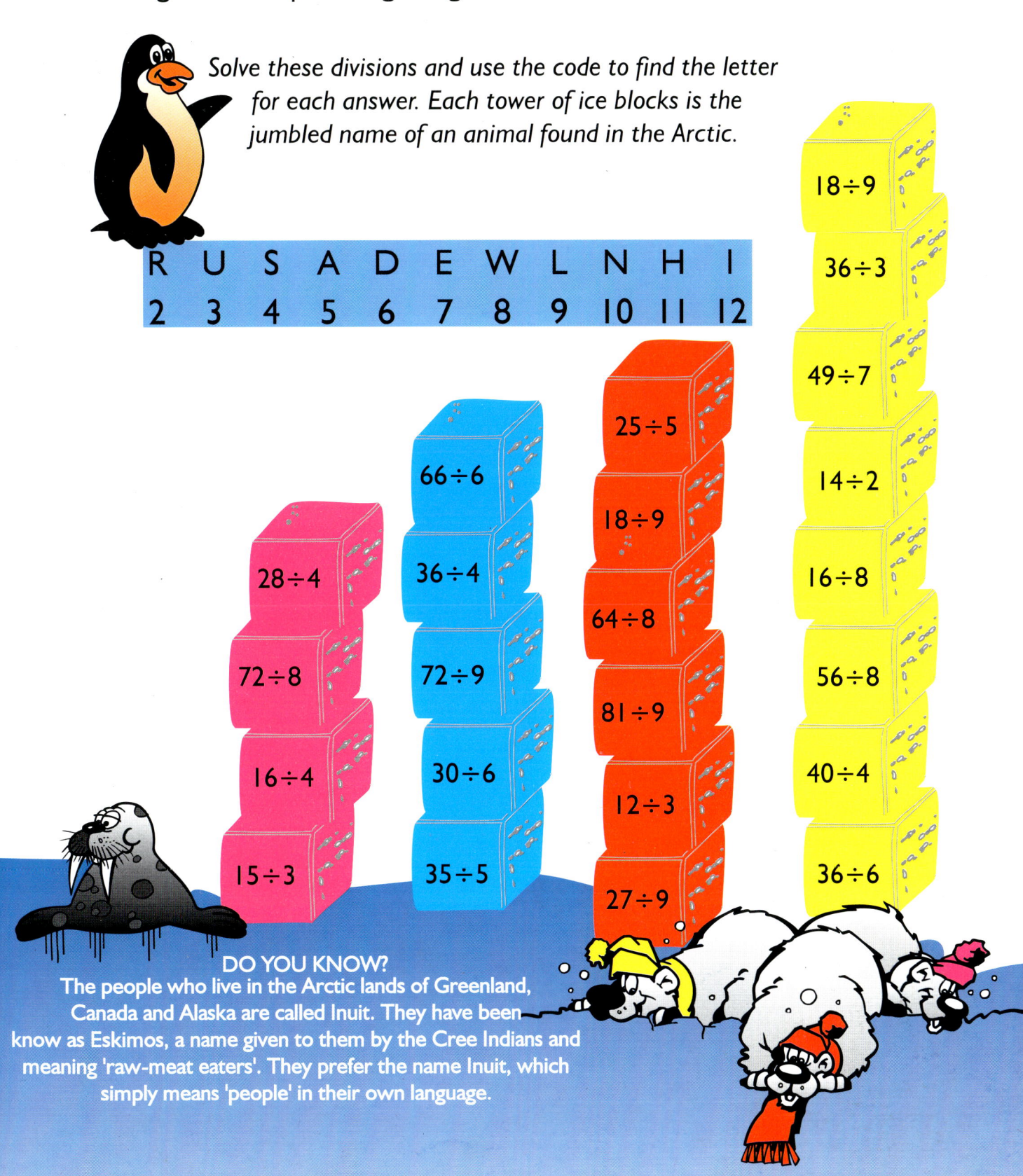

Solve these divisions and use the code to find the letter for each answer. Each tower of ice blocks is the jumbled name of an animal found in the Arctic.

R	U	S	A	D	E	W	L	N	H	I
2	3	4	5	6	7	8	9	10	11	12

28÷4
72÷8
16÷4
15÷3

66÷6
36÷4
72÷9
30÷6
35÷5

25÷5
18÷9
64÷8
81÷9
12÷3
27÷9

18÷9
36÷3
49÷7
14÷2
16÷8
56÷8
40÷4
36÷6

DO YOU KNOW?

The people who live in the Arctic lands of Greenland, Canada and Alaska are called Inuit. They have been know as Eskimos, a name given to them by the Cree Indians and meaning 'raw-meat eaters'. They prefer the name Inuit, which simply means 'people' in their own language.

Cowboys

Find the four-letter word which is hidden in each of the sentences below about cowboys. Each four-letter word can be found by looking carefully at the letters at the end of one word and those at the beginning of the next word.

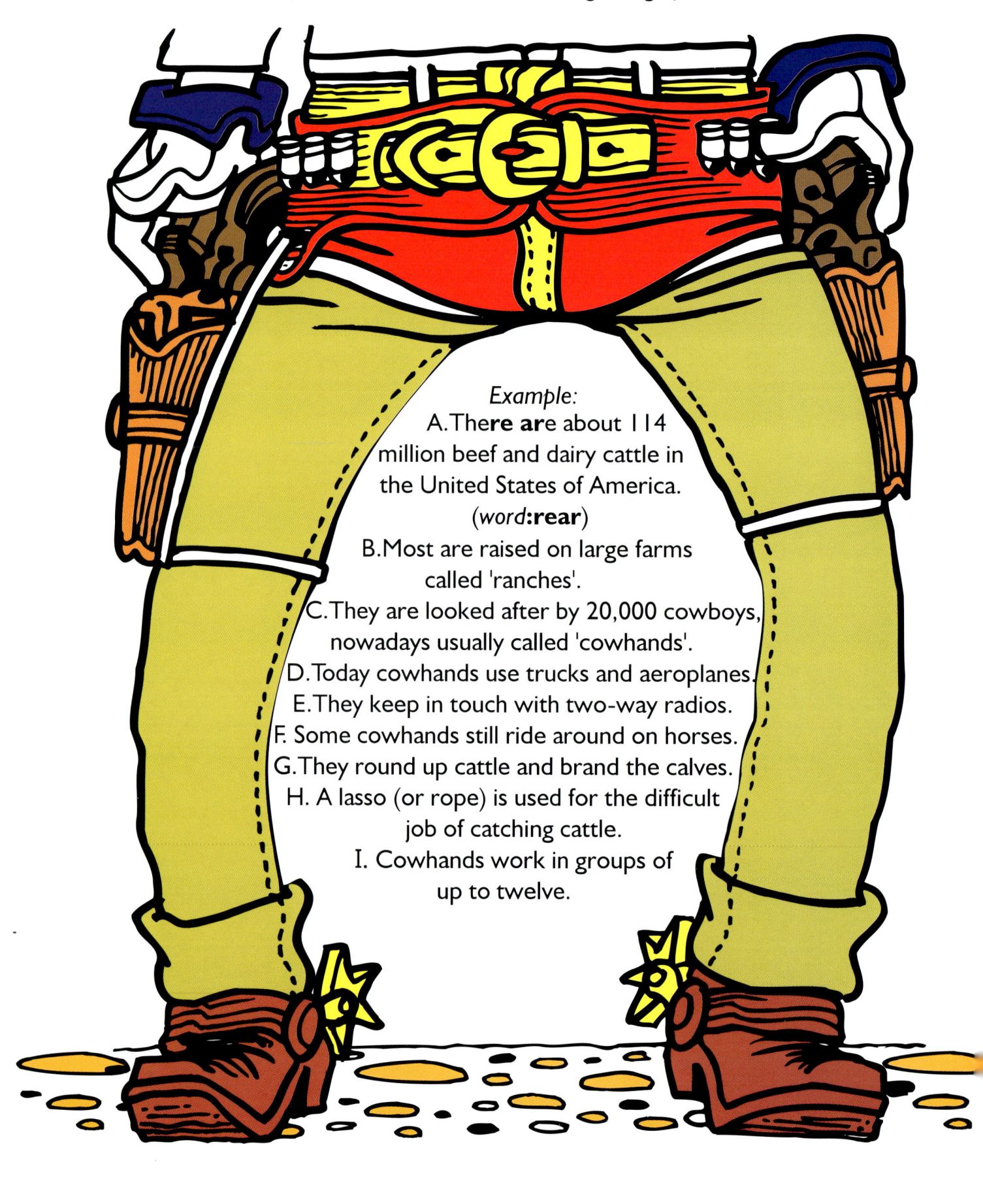

Example:
A. The**re ar**e about 114 million beef and dairy cattle in the United States of America.
(*word:***rear**)
B. Most are raised on large farms called 'ranches'.
C. They are looked after by 20,000 cowboys, nowadays usually called 'cowhands'.
D. Today cowhands use trucks and aeroplanes.
E. They keep in touch with two-way radios.
F. Some cowhands still ride around on horses.
G. They round up cattle and brand the calves.
H. A lasso (or rope) is used for the difficult job of catching cattle.
I. Cowhands work in groups of up to twelve.

Native Americans

Before Europeans arrived in North America there were many different Indian nations living there.

Some Indians, including the Haida, living on islands off the coast of North America, carved totem poles to record their family history. They went to sea in canoes to hunt whales.

Other Indians, such as Sioux, Cheyenne and Comanche, lived in the Great Plains of central North America and hunted buffalo. They lived in tepees, or tents, made of buffalo skin. They fiercely defended their lands against the invading 'white men'.

Each number in this code is a different letter. Find which series of numbers spells out the name of each of these Indian nations.

3122	CHEYENNE
36214522	CREE
36272882	CHEROKEE

Now work out what this number code means.

36235 6212

Stripey sums

To find the colours of these flags work out the multiplication problems. Use the code to find the colour of the stripe. Colour in the flags.

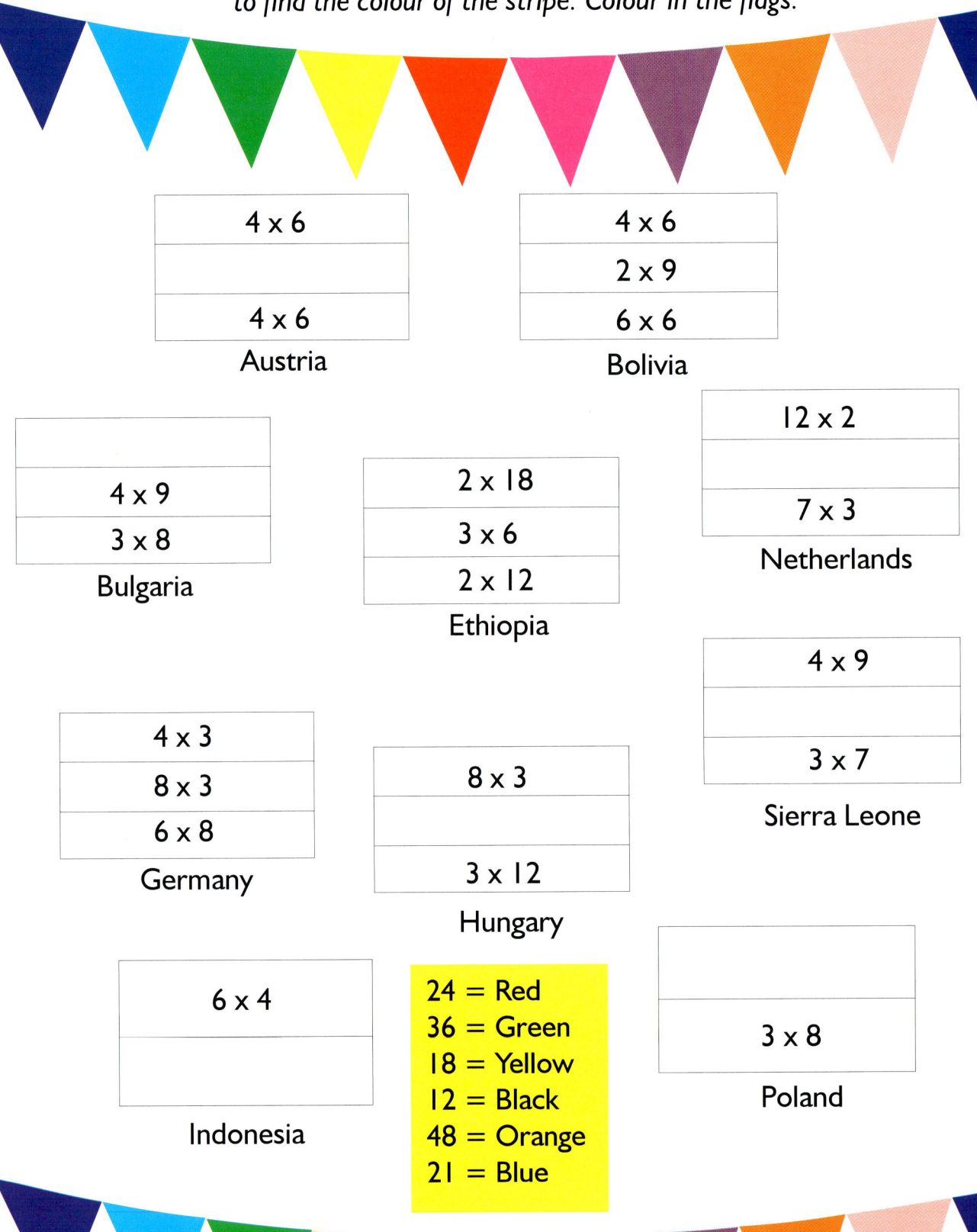

Austria
4 x 6
4 x 6

Bolivia
4 x 6
2 x 9
6 x 6

Bulgaria
4 x 9
3 x 8

Ethiopia
2 x 18
3 x 6
2 x 12

Netherlands
12 x 2
7 x 3

Germany
4 x 3
8 x 3
6 x 8

Hungary
8 x 3
3 x 12

Sierra Leone
4 x 9
3 x 7

Indonesia
6 x 4

Poland
3 x 8

Code:
- 24 = Red
- 36 = Green
- 18 = Yellow
- 12 = Black
- 48 = Orange
- 21 = Blue

Flag flying

Here is a design for a new flag. Only half of it has been drawn. The flag is symmetrical. Draw the other half of the flag.

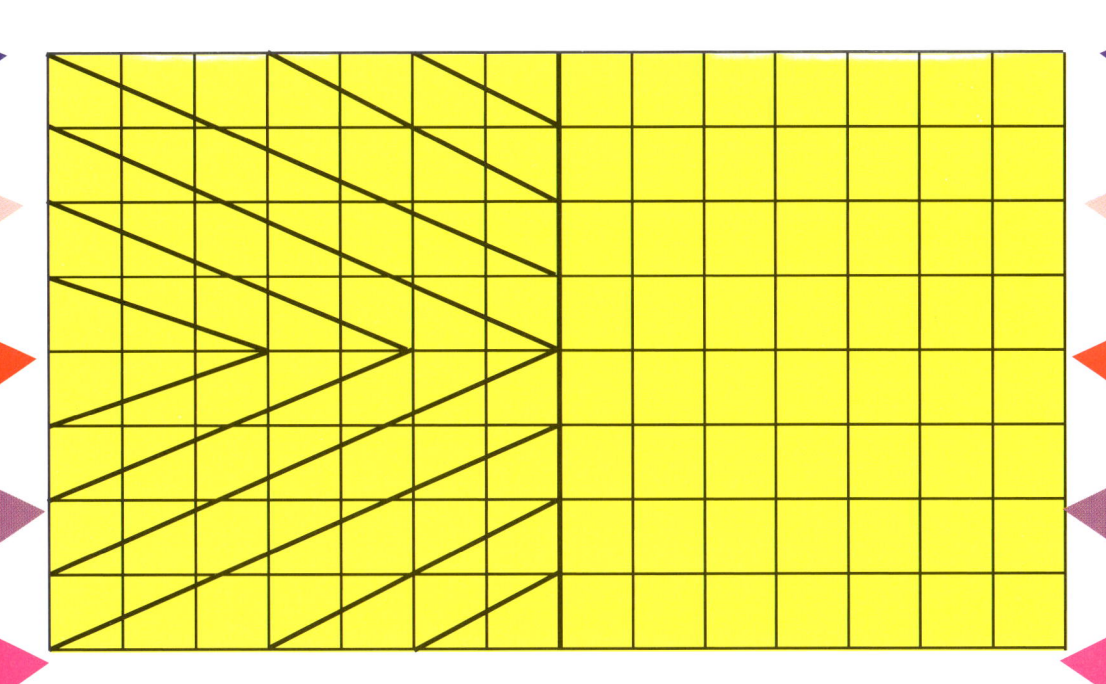

DO YOU KNOW?

There are rules for flying flags. A flag is always flown at the top of the mast, except when it is flown half-way up the mast as a sign of mourning when someone important dies. A flag flown upside down is a sign of distress. Flags are hoisted quickly and lowered slowly, often with a ceremony.

Coin conundrum

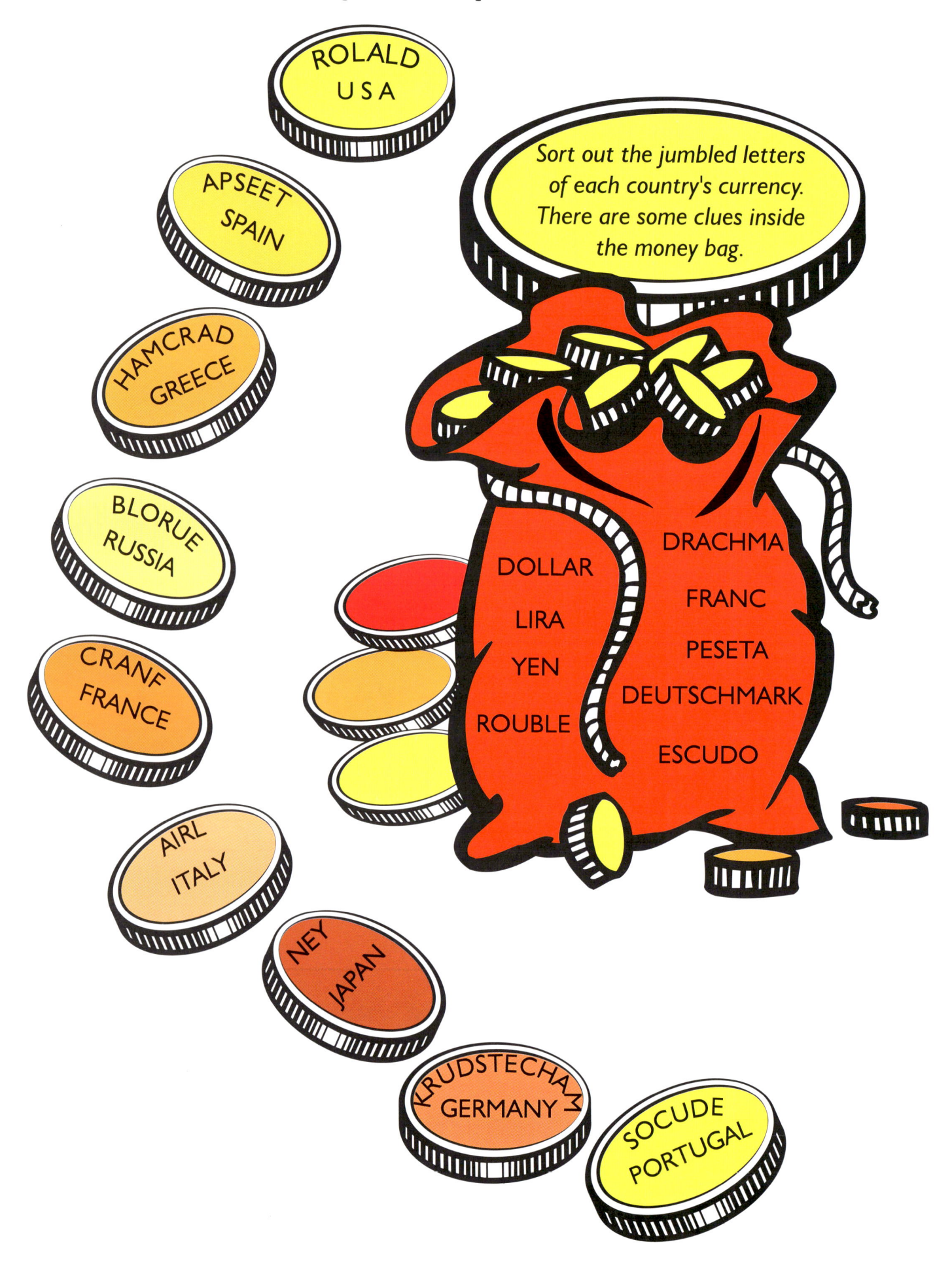

Sort out the jumbled letters of each country's currency. There are some clues inside the money bag.

- ROLALD — USA
- APSEET — SPAIN
- HAMCRAD — GREECE
- BLORUE — RUSSIA
- CRANF — FRANCE
- AIRL — ITALY
- NEY — JAPAN
- KRUDSTECHAM — GERMANY
- SOCUDE — PORTUGAL

Clues in the money bag:
DOLLAR, LIRA, YEN, ROUBLE, DRACHMA, FRANC, PESETA, DEUTSCHMARK, ESCUDO

All change

A graph can be used to work out how many German marks (DM) and US dollars ($) you get for English pounds (£).

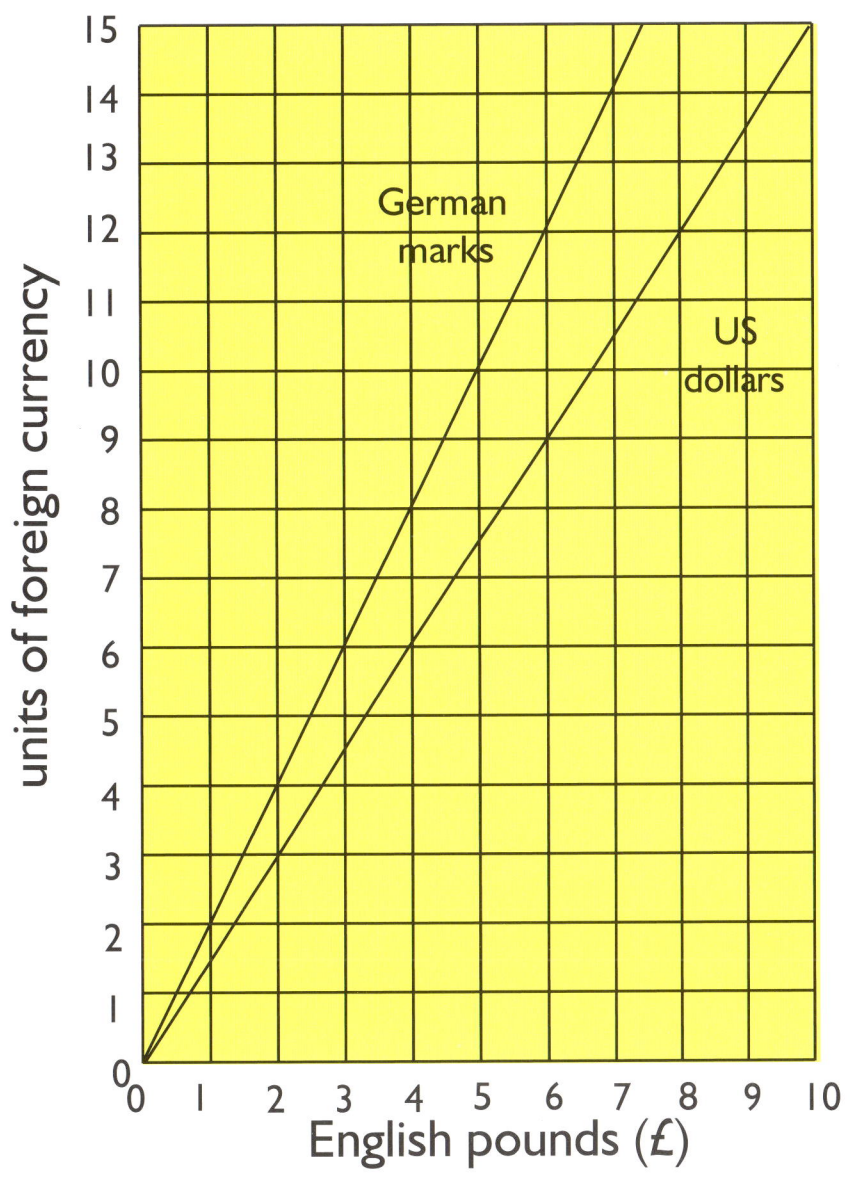

units of foreign currency vs *English pounds (£)* — graph showing two lines: German marks and US dollars.

Work out how many US dollars you get for:

£2 £6 £8 £10 £24

Work out how many German marks you get for:

£1 £5 £10 £23

How many pounds would you get for these US dollars?

$6 $12 $24

Rates of exchange for foreign currency can change daily.

Worldwide wordsearch

```
A T L A M Y L A T I A J N T
Z B E A I R E G I N I O S Y
R I N D O N E S I A D R U A
A J E N X S R I J A N D D W
D I M A U S T R A L I A A R
P F E G O N I A P S R N N O
O P Y U C H I N A I A L E N
I R O H U A Q J N F Q A O A
H S I L B L A I R Y S G C N
T L R N A W I A T R A U I A
E R J A Z N N U D Y F T X H
N C N F E C D Y N A M R E G
T P Y G E L N E P A L O M N
C W A E R O K S U R E P I H
```

*Go forwards, backwards, up, down and diagonally.
Find all these words:*

CHINA	CHILE	MALTA
JAPAN	EGYPT	NIGERIA
AUSTRALIA	MEXICO	NORWAY
ISRAEL	YEMEN	FRANCE
KOREA	ITALY	GERMANY
CUBA	IRAN	JORDAN
INDIA	PERU	SUDAN
SPAIN	UGANDA	IRAQ
PORTUGAL	POLAND	FIJI
TAIWAN	INDONESIA	NEPAL
KENYA	GHANA	SYRIA

Capital criss-cross

Here are a list of capital cities. Put each with its country.

PARIS, ATHENS, OTTAWA, LISBON, VIENNA, CANBERRA, BERLIN.

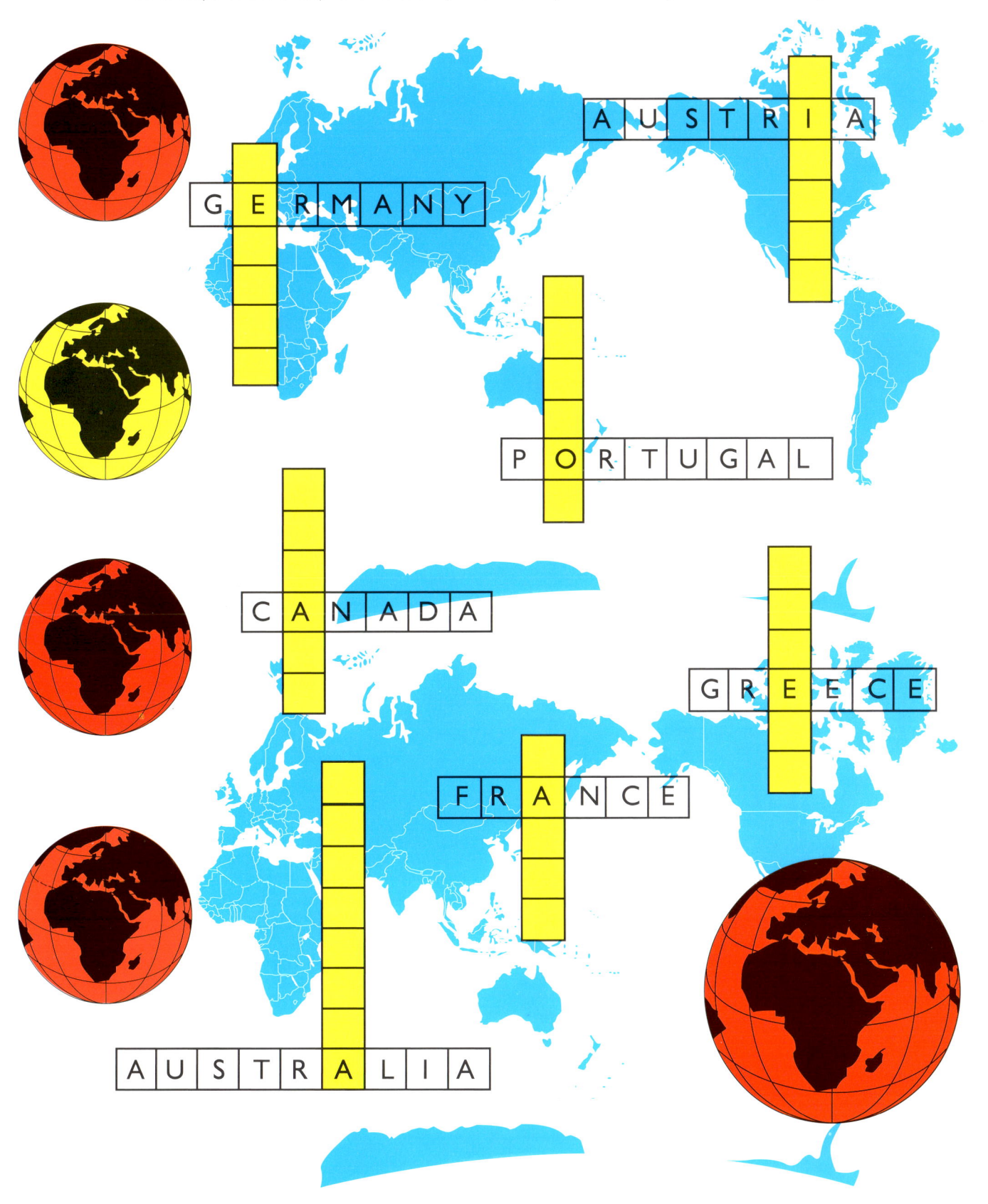

AUSTRIA	
GERMANY	
PORTUGAL	
CANADA	GREECE
	FRANCE
AUSTRALIA	

ANSWERS

People power
17, 27, 56, 79, 844, 2, 123, 24, 81, 1114, 105, 40, 9, 20, 250, 57, 30, (all in millions).

Alphabetics
Most, most, some.

Lost languages
Dutch, French, German, Hebrew, Chinese, Spanish, Greek, Japanese, Italian, Russian, Portuguese, Arabic, English.

Holiday hotel
A: Stella, B: Paradise, C: Apollo. 19 Jul-8 Aug, 4 Oct-10 Oct. Paradise,£100; Apollo,£138; Stella,£106.

Travel time
0817, John waits 4h 10mins. Wesley will catch the 0847 from Meadowlands. The quickest is the 0850.

Desert test
All false!

Sight-seeing
Eiffel Tower, Paris; Colosseum, Rome; Big Ben, London; Brandenburg Gate, Berlin.

ANSWERS

Cool co-ordinates
Mt Erebus, Mt Markham, Mt Kilpatrick, Mt Menzies.

Freeze-up
Seal, whale, walrus, reindeer.

Cowboys
B:star, C:daft, D:sand, E:pint, F:dear, G:lean, H:fort, I:king.

Native Americans
Cree, Cherokee, Cheyenne.
Check here.

Stripey sums
Austria 24,24; Bolivia 24,18,36; Bulgaria 36,24; Ethiopia 36,18,24; Netherlands 24,21; Germany 12,24,48; Hungary 24,36; Sierra Leone 36,21; Indonesia 24; Poland 24.

All change
$3, $9, $12, $15, $36. 2DM, 10DM, 20DM, 46DM.
£4, £8, £16.

Coin Conundrum
USA, dollar; Spain, peseta; Greece, drachma; Russia, rouble; France, franc; Italy, lira; Japan, yen; Germany, deutschmark; Portugal, escudo.

Capital criss-cross
Germany, Berlin; Austria, Vienna; Portugal, Lisbon; Canada, Ottawa; Greece, Athens; France, Paris; Australia, Canberra.

CLUES

People power
All numbers with 500,000 or more are rounded up to a million. All numbers with 499,999 or less are rounded down.
e.g. 1,500,000 becomes 2,000,000
    1,499,999 becomes 1,000,000

Lost languages
Think of some languages and see if you can find them amongst the jumbled groups of letters.

Holiday hotel
The more special a hotel sounds in the description the more expensive it will be.

Travel time
John leaves at 7.50 and arrives at Greenfields 30 minutes later at 8.20. Wesley will arrive at Greenfields or Meadowlands at 8.40.

Sight-seeing
The information about each sight already has a clue to help you. Here are some extra clues:
The people watching in the Colosseum were Romans. The Houses of Parliament is the place where you find the British government. Britain fought Germany in World War 2.

Cool co-ordinates
Don't forget when using pairs of co-ordinates to go along and then up.

Cowboys
Here are some clues to help you find the words.
B: it twinkles in the sky
C: means stupid
D: you find it by the sea
E: a bottle of milk
F: rhymes with clear
G: rhymes with mean
H: soldiers fight in this place
I: married to a queen

Native Americans
The four letter name, CREE, must be the four numbers 3122. So EE must be 22. Now work out the others. Then you can work out which number each letter must be.

All change
Make sure you use the right line for the dollars and marks problems. When you need to change more pounds than are shown on the graph, work out a smaller amount and then multiply, e.g. for £20 worth of dollars, look up £10 worth of dollars and multiply by two.